THE *Carluccio's* COLLECTION

MEAT, POULTRY & GAME

ANTONIO & PRISCILLA CARLUCCIO

Dedicated to the memory of
photographer André Martin

QUADRILLE

Contents

Foreword   4

Meat   10

Poultry and Game   40

Glossary of Meat Poultry
   and Game   54

Index   63

All recipes are for 4 unless otherwise stated. Use either
all metric or all imperial measures, as the two are not
necessarily interchangeable.

Foreword

It is said that Italians eat anything that moves or flies but doesn't talk. I have analysed this myth and indeed they do. Beef, pork, horse, donkey, poultry, sheep, goat, rabbit, pheasant, hare, venison, wild boar and even little birds are all part of the Italian meat larder. Not only this, but Italians also eat most animals' insides – for example almost the whole of their beloved pig is used in the kitchen, leaving the few inedible parts to be used by the cosmetic industry.

The fascinating aspect of all this is that Italians are equally fond of meat and vegetables – they eat every variety of meat in different forms but in moderate quantities, preferring to put the emphasis on quality and variety. The Italian meal is usually divided into three or four courses, so it is not necessary to have a big lump of meat as a main course.

The raising of animals first took place in areas where geographical and environmental conditions were best suited to supporting agriculture. The entire arch of the Alps and pre-Alps – the hilly and mountainous parts of Italy that spread over Liguria, Piedmont, Lombardy and Veneto, and the Apennines – are the backbone of Italy from North to South, and are ideal for raising grazing animals, such as beef cattle, sheep and goats. The flat parts of Italy, like the very fertile Po Valley, are more suited to pork and all kinds of poultry. Sheep and goats are also raised in the bushy and wild areas of Tuscany, Umbria,

Marche, Campania, Calabria, Puglia and the islands, but these regions are mainly considered as the natural habitat of wild animals, from wild boar to all sorts of game – which Italians love in season.

The historical inheritance from north to south, the countless invasions of all sorts of civilizations and the constant travel and empire-building of the Romans have left deep-rooted culinary traditions that are still visible today in the regional cuisines. In Piedmont the very special *sanato* or *vitellone* beef is often eaten raw, after having been marinated for a couple of hours in olive oil, garlic and lemon juice. Venetian *carpaccio* has now lent its name, both in Italy and abroad, to all sorts of dishes based not only on raw beef – as in the original dish – but also on thinly cut fish and even vegetables. The Ligurians are much more into game, like rabbit, flavoured with the local olive oil and olives. Emilia Romagna is the pork region *par excellence* – just think of Parma Ham and all the various wonderful salami that are eaten fresh in endless recipes.

Although in every big city there is at least one butcher that sells horse and donkey meat – which, by law, has to be separated from other meats – only a minority of people eat them, although they are said to contain plenty of goodies that are beneficial to the body. I was once invited to a very posh restaurant in Emilia Romagna where I had to try a dish of raw minced foal – for professional reasons! – and my wife did not talk to me for three days!

As far as eating 'oddities' goes, Italians – like the French – see only their culinary value and not the sensationalistic aspect. Tripe, trotters, the whole pluck of lamb or pork, and even the entrails of milk-fed lambs are specialities of great culinary interest. All these bits and pieces used to be the cheapest cuts destined for the poor people; today such dishes are greatly appreciated for their originality by rich and poor alike, although now they can command quite a high price.

Italians are not squeamish, and their upbringing makes them happy to eat all sorts of things without thinking too much about it or becoming a vegetarian as a protest. However, modern society is more sensitive to certain environmental issues and so the practice of eating small birds, for instance, is rapidly disappearing as people are increasingly critical of the inhumane raising or killing of animals. After all, our society offers so many alternatives that surely it is time to change.

Enjoy this book of the best-known and most appreciated genuine Italian meat dishes and you will discover a whole new world of taste.

Antonio Carluccio

Stracotto

BRAISED BEEF

Braised Beef

In Italy brasato *or* braciato *are the terms used to describe dishes of pieces of beef slowly braised in wine with carrots, onions, celery and spices.* Brasato, *typical of Northern Italy (especially Piedmont and Lombardy), is usually made with* manzo *(mature beef), and takes about 2 hours to cook. It is normally eaten in slices accompanied by vegetables.*

Stracotto, from the word for overcooked, describes a piece of beef cooked for even longer – at least 3 hours – in a slow oven until the meat is very tender. The other ingredients include red wine, celery, carrots, onion and a few tomatoes.

4 tbsp olive oil

a nice piece of beef such as rump or brisket, with a little fat, weighing about 1.5 kg (3¼ lb)

2 carrots, cut into very small cubes

1 large onion, finely chopped

3 celery stalks, cut into small cubes

10 juniper berries

20 peppercorns

a few bay leaves

100 g (3½ oz) fatty Parma ham, cut into thin strips

1 litre (1¾ pints) dry white wine

1 litre (1¾ pints) beef stock

salt

45 g (1½ oz) butter

Heat the olive oil in a large, preferably cast iron, pan, add the beef and brown on each side, then remove from the pan and set aside.

Add the carrots, onion, celery, juniper berries, peppercorns, bay leaves and Parma ham and fry until the vegetables are soft. Return the meat to the pan and add the wine, stock and a little salt. Bring to the boil, then reduce the heat, cover and cook slowly until the meat is very tender, about 2 hours. Pierce the meat with a skewer to check if it is well cooked; if necessary, cook for a little longer. By the end of the cooking time most of the liquid should have evaporated.

Remove the meat from the pan, whisk in the butter and add a little more stock or wine – enough to bring it to a velvety consistency.

Serve the meat thinly sliced, accompanied by the sieved sauce.

Arancini di Riso alla Palermitana

RICE BALLS PALERMO-STYLE

350 g (12 oz) minced beef

½ recipe quantity of Neapolitan Tomato Sauce (see right)

800 g (1¾ lb) risotto rice, such as carnaroli or arborio

6 eggs

1 tbsp finely chopped flat-leaf parsley

100 g (3½ oz) hard pecorino cheese, grated

150 g (5 oz) soft caciocavallo cheese, cut into small cubes

salt and pepper

flour for dusting

dried breadcrumbs for coating

olive oil for deep-frying

Cook the beef in the tomato sauce for 30 minutes, then season to taste.

Cook the rice in 2 litres (3½ pints) of lightly salted boiling water for 12 minutes only. Drain, spread out on a work surface and leave to cool.

Beat 4 of the eggs with the parsley and pecorino and mix thoroughly with the rice. Thickly cover the palm of your hand with some of the mixture. Put a tablespoon of the meat sauce and a little caciocavallo in the centre. Close your hand and seal with a little more rice to make a ball the size of a small orange. Repeat with the rest of the mixture.

Beat the remaining eggs. Roll the balls in flour, then in the beaten egg and finally in the breadcrumbs. Deep-fry in plenty of olive oil for about 5 minutes, until golden brown. To achieve more crispness, after frying you can bake them for 5 minutes in an oven preheated to 230°C/450°F/gas8. In bars they are wrapped in a napkin and eaten standing up and with your hands. They are fantastic cold for picnics. Makes 20

Neapolitan Tomato Sauce

Naples is synonymous with spaghetti, pizza and naturally, therefore, with one of the basic tomato sauces. Salsa di Pomodoro alla Napoletana is known not only in Italy but also everywhere in the world a Neapolitan immigrant has set up a business. It is indeed a delightful sauce, usually prepared with sun-ripened tomatoes. During winter, however, tinned or bottled tomato pulp is used. Some people prefer to cook the sauce for only about 5 minutes if the tomatoes are very ripe, while others let it simmer for 20–30 minutes for a more concentrated flavour, even adding a spoonful of tomato paste.

Heat 90 ml (3 fl oz) extra-virgin olive oil in a pan and gently fry 2 crushed garlic cloves for a few minutes without allowing it to colour. Add 1 kg (2¼ lb) ripe tomatoes, peeled, deseeded and chopped, and fry, stirring constantly, for 5 minutes, allowing just the excess liquid to evaporate. Add 6 torn basil leaves and salt and pepper to taste and the sauce is ready to use for the most wonderful plate of spaghetti or many other dishes.

Arrosto di Vitello al Latte

MILK-ROAST VEAL

55 g (1 ¾ oz) butter
1.5 kg (3 ¼ lb) lean silverside or topside of veal
100 g (3 ½ oz) parma ham, cut into smal! strips
pinch of freshly grated nutmeg
salt and pepper
about 2 litres (3 ½ pints) milk

Melt the butter in a large pan into which the veal will just fit snugly.
Add the meat and brown on all sides. Add the Parma ham strips, grate
over the nutmeg and season with salt and pepper.

Pour in just enough of the milk to cover the meat by two-thirds.
Cover and simmer gently for about 2–2½ hours, until tender, topping
up with more milk from time to time to prevent the meat drying out.
Serves 6-8

This is a very delicate dish, which should be
served cut into thin slices and accompanied by
green beans, Swiss chard or spinach. It is also
delicious served cold with a salad, and leftovers
may be minced to use as a stuffing for ravioli.

Veal

*After pork, the veal from milk-fed calves is
the most important meat in Italian cooking.*

*All the cuts are used to produce the
most varied dishes: cubed in stews with a
little white sauce it becomes a* spezzatino,
similar to French blanquette de veau. *The
most popular cut is the* paillard, *a large thin
slice of veal, which is seared on the griddle
for a minute on each side or dipped in
beaten egg and breadcrumbs and then fried
as* cotoletta alla milanese. Saltimbocca *is a
speciality of Rome, with the veal slices
covered with just a slice of ham and some
sage leaves and fried. Rolled and stuffed
with pancetta, they become* uccelli scappati
(*'flown-away birds'*), *a speciality of
Reggio Emilia. Of course, we must not for-
get* scaloppine al limone, *with Marsala and
lemon juice, and Ossobuco alla Milanese
(overleaf), just to mention a few of the
regional dishes made with veal.*

Ossobuco alla Milanese
SHIN OF VEAL MILANESE-STYLE

1.25 kg (2½ lb) shin of veal, cut into 4 cm (1½ in) lengths, with the
    marrow bone in the centre
about 4 tbsp olive oil
1 onion, diced
2 celery stalks, diced
1 carrot, diced
2 glasses of dry white wine
about 300 ml (½ pint) veal stock
salt and pepper
seasoned flour for dusting
FOR THE GREMOLADA:
thinly pared rind of 1 lemon, finely chopped
1 garlic clove, finely chopped
large handful of parsley, finely chopped

Dust the veal shin with seasoned flour. Heat the olive oil in a large
pan, add the meat and brown it on all sides. Remove from the pan and
set aside.

Adding more oil if necessary, gently fry the onion, celery and carrot
in the same pan until lightly browned. Return the meat to the pan,
pour in the wine and stock and bring gently to the boil. Cover and cook
for about 1½ hours, until the meat is tender, removing the lid towards
the end of cooking. Check from time to time and add a little more
stock if the mixture is getting too dry.

Make the *gremolada* by mixing the ingredients.

Adjust the seasoning of the *ossobuco* and serve with Risotto allo
Zafferano (see opposite) and the *gremolada*.

Risotto allo Zafferano

SAFFRON RISOTTO

1.75 litres (3 pints) vegetable stock
10 strands of saffron or 3 small sachets of saffron powder
1 small onion, finely chopped
4 tbsp olive oil
85 g (3 oz) butter
350 g (12 oz) risotto rice, such as arborio or vialone nano
salt and pepper

Add the saffron to the stock, bring to just below the boil and keep it at a gentle simmer.

In a separate large heavy-based pan, sweat the chopped onion in half the butter and the olive oil and cook until the onion is soft. Stir in the rice and stir it well to ensure all the grains are coated in the oil and butter.

Then start to add the stock. Start by adding a ladleful at a time, stirring continuously, for about 15 minutes. When most of the stock has been used, test a grain of rice to check its consistency and add more stock as necessary. The rice is done when it is tender on the outside but has a firm bite in the centre. Be sure to take the rice off the heat just before you think it is ready because it will continue to cook in its own heat. The ideal consistency for risotto is soft and runny (you should be able to pick it up with a fork). Risotto should never be cooked until it is solid.

Finally, add the remaining butter, season to taste and beat the risotto energetically to make sure all the ingredients are thoroughly mixed and the risotto looks creamy and shiny.

Serve on warmed plates.

Nodino di Vitello al Salvia

VEAL CUTLETS WITH SAGE

4 tenderloin veal chops, each weighing about 250 g (9 oz)

flour for dusting

85 g (3 oz) butter

4 sprigs of sage

1 glass of dry white wine

25 g (¾ oz) salted capers, soaked in water for 10 minutes, then drained
and finely chopped

zest of 1 lemon

1 tbsp finely chopped flat-leaf parsley

salt and pepper

Dust the chops with flour on both sides. Heat the butter in a frying pan and gently fry the chops, 2 at a time if necessary, for 15 minutes on each side, until well browned.

Remove from the pan, add the leaves from the sage sprigs and pour in the wine. Bring to the boil, stirring to scrape up the sediment from the base of the pan, then add the capers, lemon zest and parsley. Reduce the heat and mix well.

Return the chops to the pan and cook gently for 10 minutes. Season with salt and pepper to taste, then serve.

Nodino is a cutlet taken from the ribs. This is one of many ways of cooking it, typical of the North where this kind of meat is mostly consumed.

Sage

Along with basil, oregano, rosemary and parsley, sage is one of the most popular herbs in Italian cooking and is used in every region. It is a perennial plant with evergreen oval leaves that are velvety to the touch. The grey-green leaves contain a fragrant oil that is delicious with white meat like veal, pork and chicken. Among the most popular ways of using sage are with calves' liver sautéed in butter and in ravioli or tortellini, along with meat and vegetables and parmesan.

Caper

The caper is a bud of a plant with very pretty thick round or oval shaped leaves. The harvesting of the buds starts in late springtime in Sicily. The smallest capers are the most sought after, because of their flavour and tenderness. The larger they grow, the less taste they have.

Like olives, capers are bitter and inedible when raw and need first to be cured before being eaten. They can be cured in either vinegar, brine or dry salt. I think the best medium is either brine or dry salt. The best way to use capers is to add them to a dish towards the end, so that they keep their flavour and do not turn bitter.

Vitello Tonnato
VEAL IN TUNA SAUCE

1 litre (1¾ pints) dry white wine
2 celery stalks, chopped
1 carrot, chopped
1 onion, chopped
1 garlic clove, chopped
a few bay leaves
1 kg (2¼ lb) veal topside or eye of silverside, tied with kitchen string
   to make a large, longish roll
salt and pepper
parsley leaves and capers, to decorate
FOR THE SAUCE:
350 g (12 oz) mayonnaise
45 g (1½ oz) salted capers, soaked in water for 10 minutes, then drained
   and very finely chopped
60 g (2 oz) pickled gherkins, very finely chopped
250 g (9 oz) tuna fish in oil, drained
2 tbsp finely chopped flat-leaf parsley

Put the wine, celery, carrot, onion, garlic and bay leaves in a large pan with the meat and add water to cover. Season. Bring to the boil, then reduce the heat and simmer for 1½ hours, until the meat is tender.

Meanwhile, mix together all the ingredients for the sauce and purée in a blender or food processor. Season to taste if necessary.

Remove the meat from the pan, take off the string and cut the meat into very thin slices. Spread them over a large serving plate and cover with the sauce. Decorate with parsley leaves and capers.

Serves 6

Piccata Milanese
VEAL WITH PARMA HAM MILANESE-STYLE

4 thin slices of veal, weighing about 125 g (4½ oz) each
65 g (2¼ oz) butter
55 g (1¾ oz) speck or parma ham, cut into small strips
flour for dusting
4 tbsp stock
1 tbsp finely chopped flat-leaf parsley
juice of 1 lemon
salt and pepper

Trim the slices of veal to a uniform shape. Heat 45 g (1½ oz) of the butter in a large pan and fry the speck or Parma ham for a few minutes. Season the veal and dust with flour, then fry in the same pan until golden on each side. Remove from the pan and keep warm.

Add the rest of the butter to the pan, then stir in the stock to loosen the bits on the base of the pan. Add the parsley and lemon juice, bring to the boil, then pour over the meat and serve immediately.

You can use chicken or turkey breast here instead of veal. What these meats have in common is that they cook very quickly and absorb the flavouring, which can also be wine.

Parma Ham

Prosciutto, probably from the Latin perexutus *meaning dried, is among the most renowned and is probably one of the best-loved foods from Italy worldwide. Prosciutto crudo is the essential ingredient in an Italian antipasto. It is eaten accompanied by either melon or figs and with grissini or good bread. It can also form part of a main course, served for example with buttered asparagus and boiled potatoes.*

Parma ham, just one of the types of prosciutto produced in Italy, is so well-known that any Italian ham is almost exclusively associated with it, although many regions produce their own local hams.

Punta di Petto d'Agnello Ripieno

STUFFED BREAST OF LAMB

1 piece of punta di petto of lamb (see below), weighing 1 kg (2¼ lb)

3 eggs, beaten

8 tbsp soft fresh breadcrumbs

1 tbsp raisins

1 garlic clove, finely chopped

1 tbsp pine nuts

60 g (2 oz) parmesan cheese, finely chopped

1 tbsp finely chopped parsley

salt and pepper

a little oil

Preheat the oven to 180°C/350°F/gas4. Slit open the breast of lamb along one side and made a pocket among the layers. Mix together the eggs, breadcrumbs, raisins, garlic, pine nuts, parmesan, parsley and some salt and pepper. Stuff the pocket with this mixture and then sew it up with a needle and kitchen string.

Brush with a little olive oil and bake in the oven for 1¼ hours. Serves 4-6

This cut, more often used for veal, is the extreme soft part of the breast of lamb, underneath the cutlets. The layers of meat and fat are ideal for making a pocket for stuffing.

Lamb, Mutton

Abbacchio *is the name given to a dish traditional in Rome at Easter. The lamb is cut into pieces and cooked in a sort of egg-and-lemon sauce, probably based on the Greek recipe* avgolemono. *The most popular flavourings with lamb in Italy are garlic, of course, thyme, rosemary and mint.*

Little baby lamb cutlets, called bistecchine *or* costolette, *are often grilled, when they are called* scottadito *('finger burn') because they are usually eaten with the hands.*

Castrato or *montone, the meat of a castrated ewe, is more popular in Southern Italy where they love a stronger taste of lamb. The meat is of an intense red colour and not so lean. It is ideal for stews but is also roasted if the animal is not too old, or even grilled with rosemary and basted with olive oil and lemon juice.* Pecora, *meat from the adult ewe, is used in the same way, but will be a little tougher. Mutton has a good flavour, but is only eaten in the south where many recipes were developed for its use in stews.*

PANE di MONTEGEMOLI
COTTO a LEGNA

1995

Risotto all'Isolana

RISOTTO ISOLA-STYLE

Luganiga Fresh Pork Sausages

These long thin fresh pork sausages were probably the ancestors of the hot dog. They are made with relatively coarsely minced pork and have a 40 per cent fat content. The minced meat is stuffed into a single piece of gut and sold by the metre, divided into long sausage segments. Such sausages are very common in Italy, especially in the Northern and Central regions where, in winter, they are eaten cooked in a tomato sauce accompanied with polenta. They can also be grilled, fried or braised. The meat can also be extracted from the gut, crumbled and fried as part of the base for a pasta sauce or a risotto. I particularly like them fried with peppers or as in Polenta Concia con Salsiccia, page 28.

300 g (10½ oz) luganiga sausage (see left) or other coarse pork sausage
1 onion, finely chopped
85 g (3½ oz) unsalted butter
400 g (14 oz) risotto rice, such as vialone nano or arborio
1 litre (1¾ pints) chicken stock
1 tsp ground cinnamon
salt and plenty of freshly ground black pepper
60 g (2 oz) parmesan cheese, grated

Take the sausage meat out of its skin and crumble it. Gently fry the meat and onion in 55 g (1½ oz) of the butter until the onion is translucent and the meat is slightly browned.

Prepare the risotto as described on page 15, then remove from the heat, add the cinnamon and the rest of the butter and stir to mix well. Serve topped with the parmesan cheese.

Isola, south of Verona, is the area from which this remarkable risotto comes. The unique use of cinnamon reflects the influence of nearby Venice, which imported spices from the East during the Middle Ages.

Zampone e Lenticchie

ZAMPONE AND LENTILS

1 precooked zampone, weighing at least 1 kg (2¼ lb),
    or 2 smaller ones
300 g (10½ oz) lentils, preferably those from
    Castelluccio
4–5 sage leaves
small sprig of rosemary
a few celery leaves
2 garlic cloves, peeled
2 sun-dried tomatoes, halved
a little peperoncino (chilli)
3 tbsp extra-virgin olive oil
salt and pepper

Put the zampone in a pan of cold water and bring to the boil, then reduce the heat and simmer for 20 minutes, or according to the instructions on the packet.

Meanwhile, put the lentils in a pan of cold water with the herbs, garlic cloves, sun-dried tomatoes and chilli. Bring to the boil and simmer for 20 minutes or until tender.

Discard the herbs and the whole garlic cloves, then add the extra-virgin olive oil and some salt and pepper to taste.

Slice the zampone across thickly and serve with the lentils.

Serves 4-6

This is a truly Emilian dish – there, thanks to the great abundance of local Parma hams, zampone – or stuffed pigs' trotters – are widely available fresh.

Tofeja del Canavese

PORK AND BEANS

1 kg (2 lb 3 oz) pigs' trotters, tail, ears, spare ribs and small cotechinos

500 g (1 lb) fresh pork skin (see Cotenna, page 57)

small sprig of rosemary, finely chopped

2 garlic cloves, finely chopped

a few sage leaves

400 g (14 oz) dried borlotti beans, soaked overnight

2 celery stalks, finely chopped

1 carrot, finely chopped

1 onion, finely chopped

5 tbsp olive oil

1 chilli, finely chopped

pinch of freshly grated nutmeg

salt and pepper

a few bay leaves

Tofeja

Tofeja is the name of the lidded terracotta pot specifically designed for cooking this very rich, but exceptionally succulent peasant dish. Canavese is the northern part of Piedmont, bordering with the Aosta Valley where I grew up. We used to eat this dish at carnevale (carnival time). All the gelatinous parts of the pig are included.

Preheat the oven to 160°C/325°F/gas3. Singe the tail and ears to remove any hairs; they should be immaculately clean. Cut the pork skin into rectangles about 7.5 x 12.5 cm (3 x 5 inches) and season. Mix together the rosemary and 1 chopped garlic clove and place a pinch of this mixture and a whole sage leaf in the middle of each piece of pork skin. Roll up and tie with kitchen string.

Put the drained borlotti beans in a large casserole. Lay the vegetables on top, then sprinkle with the oil, chilli, nutmeg and some salt and pepper. Top this with all the meats and the pork skin rolls and cover with cold water. Scatter over the bay leaves and the remaining chopped garlic clove. Cover and bake, undisturbed, for 3–3½ hours.

Serves 8-10

Polenta Concia con Salsiccia

DRESSED POLENTA WITH SAUSAGE

Polenta

In Roman times polenta was a porridge made from the flour of various grains and pulses, such as broad beans, spelt, etc. Today the name usually refers to a porridge of yellow or white maize flour. Polenta can, however, be used to describe any type of porridge as long as the grain or pulse of origin is used to specify what it is made from, i.e. polenta di fagioli *(bean polenta).*

Polenta is best made in a copper pan by cooking the maize flour with water until it achieves a fairly solid consistency. It takes about 40 minutes to cook, depending on the coarseness of the grains, and requires constant energetic stirring to prevent it from sticking to the pan. The polenta can then be poured on to a wooden board and served in the middle of the table, where everyone can take as much as they like.

An easy-cook variety called polenta svelta *has been created in order to reduce the cooking time. It is made by pre-cooking ordinary polenta, which is then dried and milled again. The results are not as tasty as the original, but it is fine when butter and cheese are added.*

25 g (¾ oz) dried porcini mushrooms

400 g (14 oz) luganiga sausage (see page 24) or other coarse
  pork sausage, cut into 10 cm (4 inch) chunks

4 tbsp olive oil

2 garlic cloves, coarsely chopped

1 small onion, thinly sliced

sprig of rosemary

1 small chilli, finely chopped

3 tbsp dry red wine

600 g (1¼ lb) tomato pulp

salt

FOR THE POLENTA CONCIA:

2 litres (3½ pints) water

25 g (¾ oz) salt

500 g (1 lb) coarse polenta

100 g (3½ oz) unsalted butter

100 g (3½ oz) parmesan cheese, grated

150 g (5 oz) fontina cheese, preferably from the Aosta Valley,
  cut into small cubes

Soak the porcini mushrooms in lukewarm water for about 30 minutes. Put the luganiga in a large pan with the oil and fry until brown on all sides. Now add the garlic, onion, rosemary and chilli and fry for 5 minutes. Drain the porcini and squeeze out the excess water, then cut them up roughly and add to the pan. Pour in the wine and bubble to evaporate, then add the tomatoes and some salt and simmer for 20 minutes. Keep warm while you prepare the polenta.

To make the polenta, bring the water to the boil with the salt. Gradually add the polenta, stirring constantly until it has all been incorporated and is lump-free. Stir constantly over not too fierce a heat for about 30 minutes, until it pulls away from the side of the pan. Add the butter, parmesan and fontina and stir well until everything has amalgamated.

There are two ways of serving this: either by the spoonful on a plate or, traditionally, by pouring the polenta on to large wooden board and leaving it to cool a little, then slicing it and putting it on the plate with the stew. Serves 6-8

Bollito Misto

MIXED BOILED MEATS

4 celery stalks, cut into chunks

3 carrots, cut into chunks

1 large onion, peeled and spiked with 4–5 cloves

a few peppercorns

1.5 kg (3¼ lb) beef brisket

1 veal tongue, weighing 600–800 g (1¼ – 1¾ lb)

1 boiling chicken, weighing 2 kg (4½ lb)

1 kg (2¼ lb) veal brisket

piece of veal cheek, weighing 500 g (1 lb)

2 cotechino sausages (see right), weighing about 300 g (10½ oz) each

salsa verde (see right) and mostarda di cremona, to serve

Put the vegetables and peppercorns in a very large pot of lightly salted water and bring to the boil. Add the beef and cook gently for 30 minutes. Then add the tongue, chicken, veal brisket and cheek and simmer for 2 hours, skimming regularly to remove any scum from the surface. (If you don't have a large enough pot for all the meat, divide the vegetables and meat between 2 pans.) Top up with boiling water if necessary to make sure the meat is always covered.

Prick the skin of the cotechino sausages with a needle, put them in a separate pan and cover with cold water. Bring to the boil and cook gently for 1–1½ hours.

When all the meats are cooked and tender, remove them from the water. Peel and trim the tongue. Slice the meats and arrange them on a large serving plate. Serve hot, accompanied by the sauces, vegetables and a little stock.

Serves 10-12

Bollito Misto

This is one of the grandest dishes of Northern Italian gastronomy, native to the regions that traditionally raise beef, veal, chicken and pork. Piedmont, Lombardy, Emilia-Romagna and the Veneto are all famous for this dish and in some regions it is sometimes called simply bollito *or* lesso *(from* lessare, *meaning to boil). The mixture should contain at least four different types of meat, including some sausages that are cooked separately. Typical meats used include brisket of beef, veal cheek and breast, capon or chicken, tongue, pork belly and stuffed or plain pigs' trotters. The sausage used is normally the* cotechino, *the wonderfully juicy spicy sausage containing pork rind that is traditional with sauerkraut.*

In Piedmont, salsa verde *or green sauce, is served with the* bollito. *This is made by blending about 6 rinsed anchovy fillets with a couple of spoonfuls of rinsed capers, a few garlic cloves, a large bunch of parsley and a few basil leaves, then stirring in just enough extra-virgin olive oil to give a nice dense sauce.*

Gran Ragù Napoletano

MEAT STEWED IN NEAPOLITAN RAGÙ

Gran Ragù Napoletano

From the French ragoût *or meat stew, the term* ragù *has been adopted for long-cooked rich sauces, especially in Emilia-Romagna for their universally renowned* ragù alla Bolognese *and in Naples for their* ragù alla napoletana, *a sauce of tomatoes, meat, herbs and other flavourings.*

The sauce is used to dress large pasta and the sliced meat is then served separately with some vegetables. The little lamb spare ribs in this recipe, known in dialect as spullicarielli, *give a meaty flavour to the sauce and, when cooked, have a little meat left on them, which you can have some fun eating with your fingers. Sometimes the various cuts of meat are replaced by* polpettone, *a meatloaf large enough to feed many people.*

90 ml (3 fl oz) olive oil

1 large onion, finely chopped

1 kg (2 lb 3 oz) beef brisket

500 g (1 lb) pork shoulder on the bone

500 g (1 lb) lamb spare ribs

1 glass of dry red wine

2 kg (2¼ lb) very ripe tomatoes, peeled, deseeded and chopped

6 tbsp tomato paste

salt and pepper

600 g (1¼ lb) rigatoni

90 g (3¼ oz) parmesan cheese, grated

Heat the oil in a large pan or casserole and fry the onion and meat until the meat is browned on all sides and the onion soft. Add the wine and reduce a little, then stir in tomatoes and tomato paste. Cover and simmer gently for 1½–2 hours, adding seasoning about halfway through.

Cook the pasta in boiling salted water until *al dente*, then drain. Dress with the sauce and serve sprinkled with the cheese. The meat is then eaten with some vegetables as a main course.

Serves 6

Not a Sunday goes by for most Neapolitans without a nice piece of meat cooked in a rich tomato sauce.

Fritto Misto alla Piemontese

PIEDMONTESE MIXED FRIED SURPRISE

6 lamb cutlets

200 g (7 oz) calves' liver, thinly sliced

200 g (7 oz) chicken breast in thin escalopes, sliced

200 g (7 oz) beef fillet in thin escalopes, sliced

2 artichoke hearts, thinly sliced

1 aubergine, thinly sliced

1 cardoon, peeled, lightly blanched and thinly sliced (optional)

2 crisp eating apples, peeled, cored and thickly sliced

12 amaretti biscuits

4 eggs, beaten

seasoned flour for dusting

olive oil for frying

lemon wedges, to serve

Leave the cutlets on the bone but beat the other meat out thinly. Dust meat, vegetables, apples and biscuits with flour and then coat in the egg. Heat a good layer of olive oil in a large frying pan and shallow-fry every-thing until golden brown, starting with the vegetables, then the apples and biscuits and finally the meat. Serve with lemon wedges.

Serves 6

True *aficionados* of this very typical

Piedmontese dish insist that it should consist

of at least 17 or 18 different fried ingredients.

Calves' Liver

Calves' liver is the most frequently used in Italy. As well as being simply fried or grilled, calves' liver is also the foundation of many recipes, including fegato alla veneziana *(see page 36) in which it is stewed with onions, and as the basis for pâtés.*

Many regions, including Puglia, Calabria and Sicily, have recipes for specialities including liver. Popular flavourings include wine, sage, parsley, garlic and balsamic vinegar (see page 37).

Trippa alla Milanese

TRIPE MILANESE-STYLE

Tripe

Tripe is a national dish in Italy and people in every region and every town, whether poor or rich, eat tripe prepared in many different ways according to their own regional traditions.

Usually onion, celery, carrots, pepper and bay leaves are the basic flavourings for tripe. After these, the tripe can be eaten with oil, lemon juice and parsley as they do in Naples. However, ingredients like rosemary, pancetta, cinnamon, tomatoes, chilli and sage are among the favourite flavourings in other regions.

Fried in lard, butter and oil and then topped with stock, tripe is also made into a moist stew, which in some cases is topped with grated parmesan cheese before serving.

150 g (5 oz) large white beans

1.25 kg (2 lb 10 oz) mixed tripe, cleaned and blanched (see page 62)

1 onion, finely chopped

1 large carrot, thinly sliced

2–3 celery stalks, thinly sliced

55 g (1¾ oz) pancetta, chopped

60 g (2 oz) butter

2 tbsp olive oil

500 g (1 lb) tomatoes, peeled, deseeded and chopped

a few bay leaves

a few sage leaves, plus more to serve

salt and pepper

a little stock if necessary

100 g (3½ oz) parmesan cheese, grated

Soak the beans in plenty of cold water overnight and then drain.

Cut the tripe into strips. Fry the onion, carrot, celery and pancetta in the butter and oil until soft. Add the tripe and cook until the moisture has evaporated, stirring often to prevent sticking. Add the tomatoes, bay leaves, sage, salt and plenty of black pepper. Cover and cook gently for 2 hours. If the mixture becomes too dry, add a little stock.

Put the beans in a separate pan, cover with water and bring to the boil. Cook for an hour or so, until tender. Drain and add to the tripe. Cook for a further 15–20 minutes or until everything is tender. Add more stock if necessary. The result should be neither soupy nor dry.

Serve sprinkled with the parmesan cheese and a few sage leaves.
Serves 6

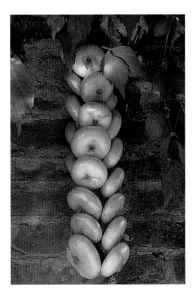

Fegato alla Veneziana
SAUTÉED CALVES' LIVER WITH ONIONS

45 g (1 ½ oz) butter
1 large onion, thinly sliced
500 g (1 lb) calves' liver, very thinly sliced
salt and pepper
finely chopped flat-leaf parsley (optional)

Heat the butter in a large frying pan, add the onion and cook until it begins to colour.

Add the slices of liver and cook until browned but still moist and pink in the centre – about 3–4 minutes on each side. If you prefer it well done, cook a little longer.

Add salt and pepper to taste and serve immediately. Some people add parsley or even a few drops of lemon juice. It is up to you.

This is another classic of Italian cuisine, this time representing the Veneto; it differs a little from Venice's version, which contains a shot of wine vinegar. As with most liver dishes, the secret of success lies in using good tender liver and only cooking it briefly.

Onion

The onion has been used for thousands of years in Italy. Introduced by the Egyptians then taken up by the Romans, it has been put to use in all sort of ways, including being fermented to make an alcoholic drink. In the Italian kitchen it is widely used in ragùs, soups and risottos. The main areas of cultivation are Sicily, Puglia, Campania and Emilia-Romagna.

The pink-and-golden-coloured onions have the most intense flavour, while the white and red are usually milder. The best red onions are those from Tropea in Calabria, which are celebrated for their sweetness.

Fegato al Balsamico

CALVES' LIVER WITH BALSAMIC VINEGAR

8 thin slices of calves' liver
flour for dusting
45 g (1 ½ oz) butter
4 tbsp balsamic vinegar
salt and pepper

Dust the slices of calves' liver with flour and shake off any excess.

Melt the butter in a large pan. As soon as it is hot, increase the heat and fry the liver very briefly – about 1½ minutes on each side.

Add the vinegar and stir to scrape up the sediment from the base of the pan.

Season the calves' liver with salt and pepper and serve immediately on warm plates.

This delightful dish is very popular in the North, especially in Emilia-Romagna where balsamic vinegar is made. You can get very good results simply using wine vinegar or even just a dash of wine.

Balsamic Vinegar

This special vinegar was once used to cure illness, hence its name balsamico, *meaning 'like a balm'. It is probably the most expensive vinegar in the world, partly because of the complex and lengthy process needed to make and mature it, and partly because only a small quantity is produced each year. Aceto Balsamico Tradizionale di Modena is the name given to the only genuine balsamic vinegar, brewed by 30 or 40 families in the Modena area who only produce 8,000 litres a year. Balsamic vinegar can be used for marinades, for brushing foods to be grilled, or to make vinaigrettes for salads or to add to sauces.*

Petti di Pollo alla Pizzaiola

BREAST OF CHICKEN IN PIZZAIOLA SAUCE

4 skinless boneless chicken breasts

4 tbsp extra-virgin olive oil

2 garlic cloves, finely chopped

1 tbsp salted capers, soaked in water for 10 minutes, then drained

1 tsp chopped flat-leaf parsley

2 anchovy fillets, chopped

500 g (1 lb) tomato pulp or chopped tomatoes

1 tbsp oregano leaves

salt and pepper

Fry the chicken breasts in the olive oil for about 8–10 minutes on each side, until brown and cooked through.

Add the garlic, capers, parsley and anchovies to the pan and fry briefly, then stir in the tomatoes, oregano and salt and pepper. Simmer for 5 minutes and then serve.

Pizzaiola sauce originally came from Naples and contains more or less the same ingredients as pizza topping, hence the name.

Chicken

In Italy there are special shops just dedicated to pollame *(poultry). The butchers are very inventive, and in their refrigerated counters you may find oven-ready stuffed breast of chicken, lovely rolled breast filled with ham, garlic, rosemary and parsley. Other parts are also skilfully prepared for cooking:* spezzatino di pollo, *cubed chicken meat ready to be cooked with tomatoes and peppers;* scaloppine *or* cotolette di pollo, *ready bread-crumbed for frying, a favourite of Lombardy; or* galantina di pollo, *boned chicken stuffed with egg, breadcrumbs, spices and herbs; or* pollo alla cacciatora, *ready to be cooked with wine and mushrooms as in Tuscany. Above all there is usually* pollo arrosto, *chicken stuffed with lemon and rosemary ready for roasting, as they do on the Amalfi coast.*

Anatra Arrosto al Prosciutto

ROAST DUCK WITH PARMA HAM

1 meaty free-range duck, weighing about 2 kg (4½ lb)

4 slices of Parma ham, with lots of fat

1 garlic clove, chopped

small sprig of rosemary

pinch of freshly grated nutmeg

salt and pepper

a little olive oil

Preheat the oven to 200°C/400°F/gas6. Singe the duck over an open flame to remove the down, if necessary.

Mince together the ham, garlic and rosemary to make a paste, then season with the nutmeg and lots of freshly ground black pepper. Rub the duck with a little oil and sprinkle with salt. Spread the paste over the breast and put the duck in a roasting tin.

Cover with foil and roast for 1 hour, then remove the foil and cook for another 30 minutes to give a golden finish.

When carving, distribute a little of the crunchy topping on to each plate with the duck meat.

This is another speciality of Emilia-Romagna, where both ducks and Parma ham are among local produce.

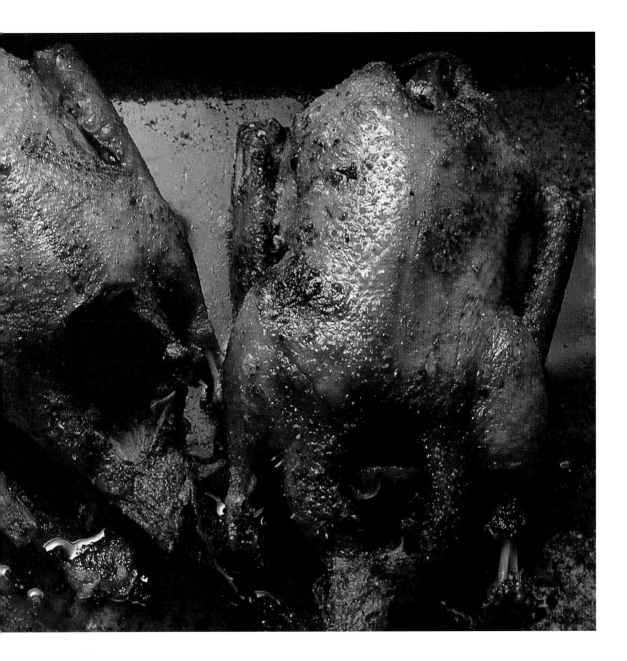

Palombacci sui Crostini
WOOD PIGEON ON TOAST

3 wood pigeons, ready cleaned, with livers

12 slices of pane di campagna (country-style white bread)

12 capers, to decorate

FOR THE MARINADE:

2 glasses of red wine

4 tbsp olive oil

a few sage leaves

1 tbsp salted capers, soaked in water for 10 minutes, then drained

1 garlic clove

3 anchovy fillets

salt and pepper

Blend all the ingredients for the marinade in a liquidizer or food processor and pour into a bowl. Add the pigeons and leave to marinate for a few hours.

Preheat the oven to 220°F/425°F/gas7. Remove the wood pigeons from the marinade and roast them for 30 minutes. Leave to cool and then remove all the flesh and the livers from the birds and discard the bones.

Put the marinade in a saucepan, add the meat and the livers and cook for 10 minutes, stirring from time to time. Transfer to a liquidizer or food processor and blend the mixture to a paste, then leave to cool.

Toast the slices of bread, spread with the paste and decorate each piece with a caper.

Makes 12

Wood Pigeon

Wood pigeon has a much higher reputation in Italy than the common pigeon. The flavour of the wood pigeon's very dark gamy meat is loved by gourmets, who enjoy this bird with equal enthusiasm whether roasted or used in sauces for dressing pasta. The diet of the wood pigeon usually consists mostly of corn and this gives their meat a particularly fine wild taste.

They are cooked much like ordinary pigeons, as long as you bear in mind that the flesh is better slightly undercooked, to make the most of its juiciness. One curious traditional way of preparing the bird is the Tuscan practice shown here of puréeing the cooked flesh to a paste and spreading this on crostini.

Quaglie allo Spiedo
QUAILS ON A SKEWER

8 meaty quails

8 rosemary sprigs

10 pieces of pane di campagna (country-style white bread), about 4 cm
(1½ inch) square and 1 cm (½ inch) thick

10 thin slices of pancetta, the same shape as the bread squares

FOR THE BASTING LIQUID:

4 tbsp olive oil

juice of 1 lemon

1 tbsp finely chopped flat-leaf parsley

2 tbsp dry Marsala

1 tsp honey

1 garlic clove, extremely finely chopped

salt and pepper

Preheat the oven to 250°C/475°F/gas9 and a wood-fired or charcoal
grill. Clean the quails and remove and discard the livers if necessary.
Insert a sprig of rosemary in each cavity and roast the birds for 15
minutes. Remove from the oven and thread them on long 2 skewers,
alternating them with the bread and pancetta.

Mix together all the ingredients for the basting liquid, adding lots of
salt and pepper. Cook the quails over the wood-fired or charcoal grill for
10–15 minutes, basting their breasts regularly with the liquid and
turning the skewers often to prevent the quails burning.

When they are golden brown, serve with the bread croûtes, which
will have collected some of the juices from the birds, and with polenta
(see page 28).

Coniglio Affogato alla Ligure

RABBIT STEW LIGURIAN-STYLE

1 rabbit, weighing about 1.5 kg (3¼ lb), cut into chunks

flour for dusting

125 ml (4 fl oz) Ligurian extra-virgin olive oil

1 large onion, thinly sliced

1 garlic clove, coarsely chopped

sprig of rosemary

a few sage leaves

small sprig of thyme

100 g (3½ oz) tasty black olives, preferably taggiasca

2 glasses of dry white wine

8 tbsp tomato pulp or passata

salt and pepper

a little stock if necessary

Wash the chunks of rabbit, pat them dry carefully then dust them with flour. Heat the oil in a large casserole and brown the pieces of rabbit on all sides.

Add the onion, garlic, herbs and olives, reduce the heat and cook until softened. Stir in the wine and bubble off some of the alcohol, then add the tomato pulp or passata and some seasoning and cook over a moderate heat for 1½ hours, until the rabbit is tender. Add a little stock if the mixture becomes too dry.

Adjust the seasoning to taste and then serve. This dish is delicious accompanied by polenta (see page 28).

Rabbit

After pork and chicken, rabbit is one of the most popular meats in Italy. Wild rabbit, coniglio selvatico, is rare as the animal is almost totally extinct from the countryside. However, the lepre or hare is still likely to be the trophy of the Italian hunter.

A small number of rabbits are kept in Italy by anyone who has the space and facilities, but most rabbit is farmed. Coniglio alla cacciatora, with mushrooms, is the best-known rabbit recipe, but rabbit ragù, made with tomatoes and served with polenta, is also a classic dish. In Liguria, the rabbit is also very much in demand, where it is cooked with the local herbs and, naturally, lots of olive oil, as opposite.

Lepre in Salmi

JUGGED HARE

1 large hare, weighing about 3 kg (6½ lb), including
    the blood

55 g (1¾ oz) plain flour

100 g (3½ oz) butter

1 onion, very finely chopped

100 g (3½ oz) pancetta, cut into small pieces

200 g (7 oz) calves' liver, cut into small strips

3 tbsp brandy

55 g (1¾ oz) bitter chocolate

salt and pepper

FOR THE MARINADE:

1 bottle of strong red wine, such as barolo

1 carrot, finely diced

1 onion, finely chopped

4 celery stalks, finely diced

1 garlic clove, smashed

a few sprigs of thyme, a few sprigs of marjoram.
    a few sage leaves, a few bay leaves

10 juniper berries

1 tsp black peppercorns, lightly crushed

Mix together all the ingredients for the marinade.
Cut the hare into large chunks, add to the marinade,
then cover and leave in the refrigerator for 24 hours.

    Remove the chunks of hare from the marinade
and pat dry, then dust them in some of the flour.
Heat the butter in a large cast iron pan and fry the

pieces of meat, a few at a time, until browned all over. Remove from the pan and set aside. Reduce the heat, add the onion and pancetta to the pan and fry until the onion begins to colour. Return the meat to the pan together with the blood, calves' liver and the marinade. Cover and cook gently for 2 hours or until the meat is tender.

Remove the pieces of hare and liver from the pan. Strain the sauce through a fine sieve and discard the solids. Mix together the brandy and just enough of the remaining flour to make a paste. Put the meat and the strained liquid back in the pan and bring to the boil. Whisk in the flour and brandy paste a little at a time to thicken. Let it boil for a minute or two, then add the chocolate, allow it to dissolve and season with salt and pepper to taste.

Serve the hare with polenta and the sauce with pappardelle. Hare cooked like this can be kept for a couple of days.

Serves 6

Typical Umbrian game country

A classic of Northern cuisine, this dish is usually served with polenta while the sauce is served separately to dress pappardelle.

Filetto di Capriolo al Barolo

FILLET OF VENISON IN BAROLO WINE

Venison

Because it tends to be dry, venison is usually first marinated in wine and olive oil. It is excellent in stews, ragùs and in pot roasts, for which the saddle is especially good. Usual added flavourings include wine, garlic and lemon.

800 g (1¾ lb) venison fillet from a large deer

flour for dusting

55 g (1¾ oz) butter

a few slices of white truffle, to serve (optional)

FOR THE MARINADE:

1 bottle of good barolo wine

4 tbsp extra-virgin olive oil

a few juniper berries

a few bay leaves

small sprig of rosemary

1 onion, thinly sliced

3–4 cloves

pinch of freshly grated nutmeg

salt and pepper

Mix together all the ingredients for the marinade. Trim the meat of gristle and skin, then add it to the marinade, cover and leave to marinate for at least 12 hours.

Remove the meat and pat dry, then cut it into medallions about 2 cm (¾ inch) thick. Put the marinade in a pan and bring to the boil, then lower the heat and boil until reduced to a third of its original volume. Pass through a fine sieve and keep warm.

Dust the medallions with flour and fry in the butter for 3 minutes on each side; they should be rare and tender.

Serve very hot with the sauce, together with polenta sprinkled with a few slices of white truffle if desired.

Serves 6

Lumachine al Sugo

SNAILS IN TOMATO SAUCE

4 tbsp olive oil

1 garlic clove, finely chopped

1 chilli, finely chopped

1 tbsp coarsely chopped flat-leaf parsley

400 g (14 oz) tomato pulp or chopped tomatoes

2 basil leaves

salt and pepper

1 kg (2¼ lb) small snails, possibly still dormant or
   closed, thoroughly washed

Heat the oil in a pan, add the garlic, chilli and parsley and fry for a few minutes. Add the tomatoes, basil leaves and snails, then cover and cook gently for 40 minutes.

Season with salt and pepper to taste and serve with a pin to remove the snails from their shells.

The small snails collected in southern Italy in autumn are best for this dish. They are a real gastronomical amusement. If you manage to get small snails, they will not need purging and cleaning.

Glossary of Meat, Poultry and Game

Agnello, Agnellone, Abbacchio / *Lamb, Mutton*
Lamb is a very Italian meat, which has been eaten there through the ages. The tradition of raising lamb has been kept alive in the central and southern regions and the islands, where the pastures give the meat a particularly good flavour. Because of the hard work involved, however, the farming of sheep for their meat has declined in the last generation.

Agnello da latte (called *abbacchio* by the Romans) are milk-fed lambs slaughtered at 3 or 4 weeks old, when their meat is very pale and tender. *Agnello* are slightly older lambs, between 9 and 12 weeks old, weighing up to 15 kg (30 lb). They are both milk-fed and reared on pasture and their flesh is both tender and flavoursome. Lambs of this size are often cooked whole on a spit. *Agnellone* are killed at about 6 months old and have very tasty meat which is mostly used in stews and *ragùs*.

Castrato or *montone*, the meat of a castrated ewe, is more popular in Southern Italy where they love a stronger taste of lamb. The meat is of an intense red colour and not so lean. It is ideal for stews but is also roasted if the animal is not too old, or even grilled with rosemary and basted with olive oil and lemon juice. *Pecora*, meat from the adult ewe, is used in the same way, but

will be a little tougher. Mutton has a good flavour, but is only eaten in the south where many recipes were developed for its use in stews.

Anatra, Anitra / *Duck*
Under these names are grouped all types of domestic or wild ducks. Whatever form it takes, however, duck is very much loved by Italians and it is much used in their cuisine, especially in the winter. Duck flesh is quite dark and gamy, and quite fatty. Always buy fresh duck as the frozen variety loses much of the quality of the meat.

The most popular variety of farmed duck is the *anatra muta*, because of its free-range lifestyle (its wings are clipped so it can't fly away, but it is left free to forage for food in ponds and the like). The main farming areas for duck in Italy are Piedmont, Lombardy, Emilia-Romagna and the Veneto. In Piedmont and Emilia-Romagna, duck are force-fed to enlarge the liver to make *fegato grasso* (foie gras), more for export to other countries where this speciality is much more appreciated.

There is also an incredible variety of wild duck, *anitra selvatica*, which is usually hunted in the autumn. It is very different to farmed duck, not only in look and taste, but also in the tenderness of

its meat. Italians do not hang wild birds for very long and in some cases, as with pheasant, they tend to cook them straight away, mostly baked or grilled. Surprisingly for such a fatty bird, duck for roasting are often barded with strips of Parma ham, but this does give an incomparable flavour.

Animelle / *Sweetbreads*
Sweetbreads are the thymus glands, and only those of young calves and lambs are normally cooked. They are used all over Italy, either sautéed, deep-fried in a breadcrumb coating or incorporated in ragùs such as Bolognese. They are also popular as stuffings for various items, including ravioli, and as part of *fritto misto*. The mild taste of sweetbreads is usually paired with lemon juice and, sometimes, sage.

To prepare sweetbreads, they must first be soaked in cold water for several hours, changing the water fairly often to eliminate any blood and impurities. They are then blanched for a few minutes in boiling water so that the nerves and veins can be easily trimmed away.

Beccaccia / *Woodcock*
The woodcock is not native to Italy, but it does fly over when migrating in spring and autumn. It has a long flat beak with brownish plumage to

camouflage it in its natural woodland habitat. Its flesh has a wonderful flavour and it is one of the best-loved wild birds. Because it cannot be farmed, it is in short supply and as a result has been over-hunted to the extent that in some parts of Italy the shooting or netting of this bird is forbidden.

Once caught, the woodcock should be hung for at least 5 days. It should only be plucked immediately before cooking. When plucking the feathers great care needs to be taken not to tear the skin, and it is also important not to wash the woodcock after plucking to retain flavour. Instead the bird should be singed over a flame to burn off any feather stubs. A small minority of purists prefer the woodcock undrawn for better flavour.

Beccaccino / Snipe

Snipe enjoys a similar gastronomic reputation as the *beccaccia* or woodcock. As with the woodcock, it cannot be raised commercially, which might in part contribute to its popularity. The snipe can be found in estuaries and lakes, where it rests while on its migration in spring and autumn. It is particularly sought after in the autumn, when it is good and fat after a summer of feeding. The dimensions of this bird are similar to that of the woodcock and, as with its cousin, one bird provides a good meal for one person. It is prepared and cooked in a similar way.

Beccafico / Fig Pecker or Blackcap

Various small birds belong to this family, which takes its name from their habit of eating figs, grapes and other juicy berries. Their meat is especially flavoursome when they feed on figs, of which they are particularly fond. They are quite rare birds and because of this their hunting is usually illegal. The majority of those sold in specialist shops come from abroad so that the consciences of the Italians who enjoy them are not troubled. The birds are prepared and cooked in the same way as sparrows. In Sicily, the name of this bird has been given to a recipe for sardines, *sardine alla beccafico*, which probably indicates that the fish should be cooked in the same way as the bird.

Budello / Intestine

Intestines are mostly used as skins and containers for salami. The gut of cows, lambs and pigs are those most frequently used by butchers, but the intestines of very young lambs are also popular because, as the animals have only been fed on milk, their guts are relatively clean. A part of veal intestines produces tripe, one of the most loved offals in Italy and for which there are many recipes (see Trippa, page 34).

Camoscio / Chamois, Wild Goat

This wild and very sprightly goat is an inhabitant of the northern Alps and Abruzzo. Its dark and very gamy flesh is treated very much as a delicacy in Italy and is particularly popular in the Aosta Valley and the Dolomites, where it lives above the tree-line high up on the hills at altitudes of 1,500-3,000 metres.

In Italy the hunting of chamois is limited because of its short supply, but frozen chamois can be bought from other countries. Although the frozen variety tends to be more tender it does not, however, have the wonderful flavour of the real thing. Incidentally, chamois leather is a by-product of this animal.

Mucetta is a special air-dried fillet of chamois which is served thinly sliced as an antipasto. This traditional method of preserving meat was a necessity for inhabitants of that part of the world as provision for the long winter months. Today, however, it is a delicacy sold at very high prices.

Cappone / Capon

The production of capon (a castrated cockerel) is almost exclusively limited to the Christmas period, when this bird is the centrepiece of the celebrations. The main regions where capons are farmed are Veneto, Emilia-Romagna, Lombardy and Piedmont.

Once castrated, it takes just six or seven months for the young cockerel to grow to an impressive 3–5 kg (6–11 lb), with extremely tender and juicy flesh. It is prepared and cooked just like a normal chicken. A particularly good way is boiling, as is done in various parts of Piedmont and Emilia-Romagna. This cooking method produces the most wonderful stock, which is used to cook tortellini. The bird itself gives a generous amount of meat that can be eaten as a part of *bollito misto* (page 31), popular all over northern Italy with *mostarda di cremona* .

Capra, Capretto / *Goat, Kid*
I myself was a shepherd when I was 13 or 14 years old. Just after the War, my father decided to buy a goat and keep it in a railway shed near the station. I was in charge of feeding the animal, which each day gave a couple of litres of milk – enough for the whole family. I certainly never wanted to eat Sisina (as she was called) and she was eventually sold when we couldn't keep her any more. Although it was not the custom to keep goats in the North, my family always had them because my parents originally came from the South, where it was quite usual.

Some goats are only good for milk, but *capretto* (kid) can also be eaten. The meat is different from that of lamb, with more of a wild taste.

Capriolo / *Roe Buck or Roe Deer*
The male of the deer family can be easily recognized by its antlers. It is a medium-sized deer with a red-brown coat that changes to grey-brown in winter. It lives in hilly woodland areas and so cannot be found in Sicily or Sardinia, but is abundant in the rest of Italy, especially in the Alps and Apennines.

I once tried *capriolo carpaccio* made with the fillet of the roe deer, which was sublime – especially as it was garnished with a few slices of truffle. The meat can also be used to make a delicious *ragù di capriolo*, with rosemary, juniper berries, nutmeg, cinnamon, anchovy and wine, which goes wonderfully well with polenta and pasta in *pappardelle al sugo di capriolo*.

Cavallo / *Horse*
Meat from both horses and donkeys (*asini*) was eaten during the War, when meat was scarce and prices high. Some Italians still have a taste for them, partly because they believe the deep red colour of the meat means it is very good for you. Few butchers still sell horse or donkey, with no more than one or two places in the major Italian cities supplying the demand of those nostalgic gourmets.

In Puglia, however, horse meat is very much in demand during the summer, especially because it is thought that the meat keeps better than that of pigs or sheep. In Puglia there exist many shops, called *equina*, where it is obvious you can only get horse meat.

Cervella / *Brains*
Brains are believed to be particularly nutritious, which is why they are given to people who need extra nourishment. In fact, brains contain a very high level of cholesterol and have less protein than the rest of the animal. It is only calves' and lambs' brains that are generally used in the kitchen.

The easiest thing is to ask your butcher to prepare the brains for you, but if this is not possible, you start by washing them in very cold water then removing all the veins and blood vessels on the surface with a small sharp knife. Next, soak the brains in water acidulated with a little lemon juice for a couple of hours, changing the water frequently. Remove the remaining membrane and any more veins before blanching them in boiling water for a few minutes.

Cervo / *Red Deer*
This most majestic of all deer is almost extinct in the wild in Italy. There are a few herds in national parks, such as Gran Paradiso in Piedmont, to remind people what Italian fauna used to be like. In addition to the attractions of its meat, venison, the deer's massive antlers have a multitude of uses.

Almost all the venison now eaten in Italy comes from Eastern Europe or from Scandinavia, where it is farmed. The deer can grow up to a weight of 350 kg (7 cwt) and its meat is one of the best and healthiest, as it is low in fat and cholesterol. Because it tends to be dry, the meat is usually first marinated in wine and olive oil.

Cinghiale / Wild Boar

Given that Italians love pork of any description, either cooked or preserved, it is not surprising that the wild version, wild boar, excites them so much. Sometimes considered a pest, boar live in the hilly woods of Tuscany, Umbria, Abruzzo, and any other area where there is thick, inaccessible undergrowth in which it can hide and feed on tender shoots and berries.

Hunting wild boar can be dangerous because this animal, when under pressure, will attack humans. Boar-hunting is, however, a major sport in the regions of Sardinia, Sicily and Calabria, and a successful hunt is accompanied by enthusiastic celebrations.

In Tuscany, wild boar is used to produce many foods, including hams, salamis and *salamini*. While fresh it is wonderful in stews and *ragùs*, and almost every Tuscan and Umbrian family keeps frozen wild boar to make a *ragù* to serve with the famous pinci pasta, hand-made giant spaghetti. Due to big demand for wild boar, many half-wild boar are farmed in enclosed woody areas leading a semi-wild life, producing a less gamy meat.

Colombo, Piccione / Pigeon

This is the domestic version of *colombaccio* (wood pigeon) and is farmed almost everywhere because of the increasing demand.

The common pigeon can be found everywhere, from the Piazza San Marco in Venice to Piazza del Duomo in Milan, not to mention London's Trafalgar Square, and it is a bird that has adapted itself to every situation. Obviously the polluted city pigeon is not really suitable for human consumption, but it is a pity considering they are magnificently fed with grain by the multitude of tourists, their meat could otherwise be particularly good.

Farmed pigeon are not only safe to eat but tasty too, even if they are not as good as the wild variety – the advantage for some is that there is no need to disguise the gamy flavour and they don't require as long cooking as the wood pigeon.

Pigeons are sold cleaned and ready for cooking and are used in famous dishes such as *piccione alle olive*, pigeon with olives, and in casseroles. You can tell the age of pigeon by the beak; the younger it is the more elastic the beak.

Coniglio / Rabbit

After pork and chicken, rabbit is one of the most popular meats in Italy. Wild rabbit, *coniglio selvatico*, is rare as the animal is almost totally extinct from the countryside. However, the *lepre* or hare is still likely to be the trophy of the Italian hunter.

Cotenna, Cotica / Pork Skin or Rind

Slightly fatty pork skin is very gelatinous and strong and is usually used for making the skins of certain types of sausage. It is also minced and used to make *zampone* or *cotechino*. In some parts of Italy, such as Piedmont, most of the fat is removed from the skin and it is then richly spiced with pepper, salt, nutmeg and parsley, rolled up, bound with string and boiled for a couple of hours until it is soft. It is usually eaten with stewed beans and a little mustard. The gelatinous taste is delicious.

Cuore / Heart

You can find lovers of heart all over Italy, although they are concentrated in the south, where offal is generally more popular. The largest heart eaten in Italy is that of the ox, although it is only used in stews because it is quite tough, while the smaller and more tender veal heart is popular cut in slices then fried or grilled. It is, however, probably the heart of the pig that is the most often used in the Italian kitchen, especially in the south where it is prepared with other offal and used in *ragù*. Lamb's heart, especially that of very young animals, is usually eaten as part of *coratella* (soupy stews of lamb pluck popular in Lazio and Umbria), but it can also be fried or stewed in wine with the rosemary, garlic and sage.

Fagiano / Pheasant

The noble pheasant was introduced to Europe from Asia during the Middle Ages. It was particularly popular in Tuscany, where its feathers were used to decorate the tables and the serving dishes whenever it appeared on the menu. The male bird is famous for his beautiful and ornate feathers, while the female looks a little drab. The male is also larger in size than his female counterpart, a fact that is important when buying a brace, a pair of birds of which one is male and the other female.

Italians do not like wild pheasant to be hung for too long and the farmed variety are not hung at all because they are so tender. Pheasant is popular in the north and centre of Italy, especially in Tuscany and Umbria, which have a culinary history in the preparation of these birds. Pheasant has a lovely gamy taste and fragrance, and the rather dark meat contains only a small quantity of fat. It is a fairly versatile bird and is often cooked in a casserole with wild berries to complement its flavour, or simply roasted in the oven after it has been rubbed well with olive oil, salt and pepper, or occasionally flavoured with some truffles.

Faraona, Gallina Faraona / Guinea Fowl

It is believed that this bird, well-known to the Greeks and Romans, was introduced from the Gulf of Guinea into Europe by Portuguese sea adventurers around the fifteenth century.

In taste, the guinea fowl has a flavour somewhere between that of the chicken and the pheasant. This bird lives wild in its country of origin, but in Italy and most of the rest of Europe it is mainly raised on farms. Its plumage is typically white spotted with grey, making it one of the most elegant and beautiful of birds.

Fegato / Liver

Liver is the best-known and most popular offal in all of Italy. It contains the important vitamins A and D, and some of the B vitamins, as well as quite a lot of iron. The livers of all domesticated animals are sought after and in some cases are quite expensive.

Naturally, like most offal, liver must be very fresh. Whichever liver you use, you must first remove and discard the fat and membrane surrounding it before cooking, as these make the liver bitter and inedible.

Ox liver is large, dark and tough. It is usually sliced and braised in wine. Calves' liver is the most frequently used in Italy and is popular for its tenderness and fine flavour. It is smaller than ox liver, although it still weighs about 2-3 kg (4½-6½ lb). As well as being simply fried or grilled, calves' liver is also the foundation of many recipes, including *fegato alla veneziana* in which it is stewed with onions, and as the basis for pâtés. Pigs' liver is also popular in Italian cooking: like ox liver it is very dark in colour, but is much smaller and has an excellent flavour.

Gallo Cedrone / Grouse

In my opinion this is the best of the game birds. Grouse is quite rare in Italy and is a protected species, so I am especially grateful to live in Britain where I can get Scottish grouse, although it is increasingly scarce here too. In Scotland, grouse nest on open moorlands, while in Italy they prefer the habitat of pine forests. Its diet of berries and insects imparts an irresistible flavour to its very dark and fleshy breast. It needs to be hung, unplucked, for at least 3 or 4 days.

Lepre / Hare

The most coveted game of the Italian hunters is the hare. Belonging to the same family as the *coniglio* or rabbit, the hare reaches the greater weight of up to 7 kg (16 lb). It differs from the wild rabbit, with which it is often confused, in that it has longer hind legs than forelegs and its meat is dark red in colour. The astuteness and speed of the hare are legendary and hunters who seek this prey without the help of a dog are rarely successful in catching it.

As the blood of the hare is a key ingredient for the marinating and cooking of the animal, it is especially important when buying hare that you check it is very fresh and properly butchered. Frozen, farm-raised hare lack this vital ingredient and, as a result, dishes cooked using them cannot match the flavour of those using their freshly butchered, wild cousins. The hanging process, especially of heavier, older animals, takes place in a marinade of blood, wine and spices (see Lepre in Salmi, page 50) and can take at least two days.

Lingua / *Tongue*

Tongue is popular all over Italy. Veal tongue is the most tender and is usually boiled and served sliced with an acidic sauce, tuna fish sauce or *salsa verde*. Tongue is also an important ingredient in a classic *bollito misto* (see page 31). To achieve the vivid red colour characteristic of the meat it needs to be pickled in a salt solution for several hours and then boiled until tender. When buying tongue, make sure it is already pickled.

Lumaca di Terra, Bovolo, Marruzelle / *Snail*

Snails are not easy to categorize as, although they are wild, they are totally different to any other game. Freshly collected snails need to be cleaned or deslimed (*spurgare*) by allowing them to feed on rusk, fresh nettle leaves and salt for a couple of days. They can then be washed and cooked in salted water. When they are done, pull the snail out of its shell, discard the black tail and wash the shell. The snails can then be used according to the recipe you are using.

I can't understand why anyone bothers with tinned snails, cooked and stuffed back in their shells, although frozen ones are acceptable.

Maiale, Maialino, Porco, Porcello, Porcellino, Porceddu, Suino / *Pig, Pork, Piglet*

Italians have always loved the pig, not only because it is so easy to raise, but because every scrap of the animal can be used. When I was a boy, almost anyone who could kept a pig, feeding it on leftovers and scraps. Today their feed is more rationalized, mixing polenta with other high-energy grains. The industry, however, feeds pigs on other less valuable grains, obtaining larger production but of a less flavoursome meat. Better quality pork is, however, still sometimes obtained from herds partly fed on the whey by-products of cheese-making, and pigs lucky enough to graze in the wild and consume foods like acorns are said to give much of the flavour to prosciutto.

As well as for their meat, pigs were also needed for their fat. Of the 200-plus kilo yield from the average pig, at least a quarter was fat and this was turned into solid and liquid lard. Today, with more information about the dangers of eating too much saturated animal fat, the pig is raised mainly for its meat and the commercially farmed pig – now available all year round – reaches an average weight of 160 kg (3 cwt).

When a pig was raised individually, it would be slaughtered in December or January so that its meat could be processed during cool weather to be preserved for use all year round. After the butcher slaughtered the pig, hams and sausages were made with the fresh meat while the perishable offal and other parts that could not be preserved were cooked for friends to celebrate the occasion.

Nothing was wasted. Even the bones, once stripped of their meat to make salami, were boiled with cabbage, potatoes and beans to make a tasty soup. The blood, which was drained from the pig to keep its meat pale, would have been used either cooked with onion or mixed with pork fat to make black pudding or *marzapane*, or even to make a dessert, *sanguin-accio*, with milk, raisins, sugar and spices. Some people still keep pigs today, but the products so loved by Italians are now usually made commercially, not from the pig in the back yard.

Italians are very fond of eating suckling pigs (*maialino, porcello* or *porcellino*) slaughtered at anything from 8 to 12 weeks of age, sometimes younger. The meat is regarded as a delicacy. In Sardinia, suckling pig is called *porceddu* and traditionally roast on a spit of *corbezzolo*, the branches of a strawberry tree, for at least 2 hours and brushed with lard from time to time. The wood fire is made of the branches of aromatic trees such as olive, juniper and myrtle to give the meat extra flavour. Suckling pigs are also baked whole in a wood-fired oven. *Porchetto or porcetto*, stuffed roast whole adult pig, is also prepared for local festivals or weddings.

Midollo, Schienale / *Marrow, Bone Marrow*

One of the attractions of *ossobuco alla milanese*, shin of beef cooked in a tomato sauce (see page 14), is the marrow. It is pure fat and tastes heavenly. Bone marrow is also used to flavour *risotto alla milanese*. When my mother cooked beef stock she used shin of beef and I would amuse myself by extracting the marrow from the cooked bone, put it on toast and season it with salt and pepper for a real treat. The round marrow that fills the length of the spinal cord is known as *midollo spinale*, *schienale* or *filone* and is considered to be quite a delicacy. It is cut into short sections and fried as part of *fritto misto alla Piemontese* (see page 33).

Oca / *Goose*

There are two types of goose raised in Italy. The first, the smaller of the two and with grey plumage, is only kept for its meat and comes mainly from Piedmont, Emilia-Romagna and Padua. The second is the Toulouse type, which can reach a weight of 10 kg (22 lb) and is especially raised for the production of *foie gras* (*fegato grasso*). In Italy, the goose used to have a similar status to the pig because, like the pig, the whole bird had a use, whether it was the meat and fat or the fattened liver and feathers.

Geese are only raised for *foie gras* in Lomellina, a small area between Lombardy and Piedmont. In this part of Italy, goose is also made into a delicious triangular salami called *salame d'oca*. The meat and fat are minced then stuffed into the skin of the long neck and then sewn up tightly. The obvious benefit is that, because it does not include pork, the salami can be eaten by those whose religious belief makes it impossible to eat pork.

Fegato grasso, the liver of force-fed geese, is also a very important product. The delicious liver can be sliced and fried or made into delicate pâtés. The French are well known for being particularly fond of their *foie gras*, but the Romans also had much appreciation for it and only now has it seen a revival in modern Italian cooking.

Goose is very similar in appearance and taste to duck, the only real culinary difference being that duck can be slightly undercooked, so that it is pink, and can be eaten cold. The fat content of goose means that it is probably only palatable when cooked all the way through and eaten warm. As with duck, goose benefits from being served or cooked with a slightly acidic sauce to offset this fattiness.

Ossobuco / *Shin of Veal*

Osso meaning bone and *buco* meaning hole, this is taken from the part of the leg where the muscle is particularly thick, giving a cut of meat about 8.5 cm (3½ inches) across cut into 2.5 cm (1 inch) thick sections with the bone and marrow in place.

Palombaccio, Colombaccio / *Wood Pigeon*

Wood pigeon has a much higher reputation in Italy than the common pigeon. The flavour of the wood pigeon's very dark gamy meat is loved by gourmets, who enjoy this bird with equal enthusiasm whether roasted or used in sauces for dressing pasta.

Colombacci sometimes mix with their city cousins when on migration, but they generally prefer to live in the woods and country-side. Farmers in some parts of the country hang up terracotta pots on their outside walls where the birds can nest. Of course, this simply makes them easier prey for their landlords. The diet of the wood pigeon consists mostly of corn and this gives their meat a particularly fine wild taste.

Wood pigeon need to be hung for a few days, so they can ripen. After this they are sold unplucked, with their giblets still intact. They need to be plucked carefully and thoroughly cleaned. The liver is especially good and so it is worth saving when the bird is drawn. The wood pigeon is generally larger than the ordinary variety and one bird makes a fine meal for one person.

Pernice / *Partridge*

There are three varieties of partridge in Italy. The most sought-after is the red-legged (*pernice rossa*), because it has the most delicate flesh and is the only variety which is still completely wild, and available from specialist suppliers only. The grey-legged (*pernice grigia* or *starna*) is less flavoursome and it is mostly raised on farms and sold commercially. The third type, the yellow-leg, can only be found in Sardinia, is similar to the red-legged variety and is equally delicious.

Wild partridges should be hung, drawn but left unplucked, for 2–3 days at least to allow the meat to tenderize and develop fully in flavour.

Pollo, Pollastrello, Pollastrina / Chicken

The chicken is the most common source of meat in the world; the reason being that it is extremely easy and economical to raise, as it is cheap to feed and quick to grow. The hen also produces eggs as well as meat. The term *pollo*, like 'chicken', is used for both the hen and cock birds and *gallo* is the name for a fully grown male or cock. Try not to think the Italians barbarians because they eat the pride of a cock, his comb. The delicious *creste di gallo* are sought by a few gourmets.

A young male cock is called *pollastrello*. *Cappone* or capon is a castrated cockerel, which grows to maturity at about between 6 and 8 months, and is sought-after for its delicate meat. *Galletto*, or poussin, is a very young cockerel which has reached the lowest possible slaughter weight of 500 g (1 lb). Due to

its tender age, it has very delicate flesh and is usually cooked spatchcocked, that is opened out and weighted to keep it flat – also known in Italy as '*al mattone*' (with a brick). I personally do not think the *galletto* worth eating because of its lack of flavour. Older male birds are, however, best boiled because they are particularly tough.

The *gallina*, or hen, is the chicken in a farm that produces eggs. After a couple of years of egg-laying, the hen is destined to end up in a pot as the basis for a good stock. In Italy, there is a saying that old chicken makes good broth (*gallina vecchia fa buon brodo*). Chicken stock, made with a 2- to 3-year-old egg-producing hen bird, is widely used in Italian cooking, but the same type of bird boiled whole makes a wonderful *brodo di gallina*, a soup which can be eaten with tagliolini or tortellini.

The best chickens are free-range and fed with maize or other grains, imparting a full wonderful flavour to the meat, which is not pale white but pinkish – with a yellow skin. In Italy there are special shops just dedicated to *pollame* (poultry).

Quaglia / Quail

This small, well-camouflaged, beige-brown bird lives wild in fields and woods and is one of the most frequently cooked of the game birds hunted in Italy. As it is easy to raise quail on farms, however, Italians do not rely on wild quail,

even if they are bigger and have a natural gamy flavour. The quail has a special place in Italian gastronomy and is much appreciated for its delicate meat and its eggs which are also used to make delicious dishes.

Farm-raised quail are sold cleaned and fresh, without being hung, ready for cooking. If using such a bird, at least a couple are needed per person and, unless it is boned and stuffed, you can eat it with your fingers. Quail can be roasted, stewed, grilled or even boiled.

Rana / Frog

Italians living in the regions of Piedmont, Lombardy, Veneto and Emilia-Romagna are well acquainted with this creature, which lives in any area where water is abundant and in Italy the rice fields of the Po Valley are the perfect place for them. Only the muscular back legs are eaten and these *coscette di rane* are sold cleaned and ready for the pot. Frogs' legs have a very delicate flavour and so they are not well suited for cooking with a lot of herbs and spices.

Rete di Maiale, Omento / Caul Fat

Caul fat is a lacy membrane of fat lining the stomach of (normally) the pig, used to bard tender pieces of meat or offal before roasting or baking and imparting a wonderful flavour to any meat. After the caul fat is taken from the stomach of